MEDICAL BREAKTHROUGHS

ANTIBIOTICS

A GRAPHIC HISTORY

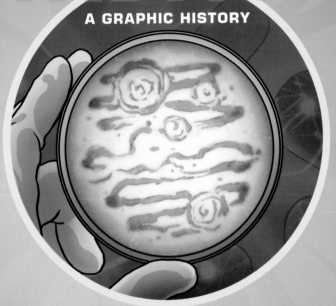

BRANDON TERRELL

ILLUSTRATED BY DANTE GINEVRA

GRAPHIC UNIVERSE™ • MINNEAPOLIS

Brandon M. Terrell (1978–2021) was a talented storyteller, authoring more than one hundred books for children. He was a passionate reader, Star Wars enthusiast, amazing father, and devoted husband. This book is dedicated in his memory—happy reading!

Graphic Universe™
An imprint of Lerner Publishing Group, Inc.
241 First Avenue North
Minneapolis, MN 55401 USA

For reading levels and more information, look up this title at www.lernerbooks.com.

Main body text is set in Dave Gibbons Lower. Typeface provided by Comicraft.

Library of Congress Cataloging-in-Publication Data

Names: Terrell, Brandon, 1978-2021 author. | Ginevra, Dante, 1976- illustrator.
Title: Antibiotics : a graphic history / Brandon Terrell ; illustrations by Dante Ginevra.
Description: Minneapolis : Graphic Universe , [2022] | Series: Medical breakthroughs |
   Includes bibliographical references and index. | Audience: Ages 8–12 | Audience:
   Grades 4–6 | Summary: "Antibiotics stop a bacterial infection from multiplying. They
   help treat pneumonia, strep throat, and much more. Their creation marked a medical
   revolution, saving lives from World War II soldiers to modern hospital patients"—
   Provided by publisher.
Identifiers: LCCN 2021014443 (print) | LCCN 2021014444 (ebook) | ISBN 9781541583917
   (library binding) | ISBN 9781728448688 (paperback) | ISBN 9781728444109 (ebook)
Subjects: LCSH: Antibiotics—Juvenile literature. | Drug resistance in microorganisms—
   Juvenile literature.
Classification: LCC RM267 .T46 2022 (print) | LCC RM267 (ebook) | DDC 615.7/922—dc23

LC record available at https://lccn.loc.gov/2021014443
LC ebook record available at https://lccn.loc.gov/2021014444

Manufactured in the United States of America
1 – CG – 12/15/21

TABLE OF CONTENTS

CHAPTER 1:
THE HISTORY OF GERMS

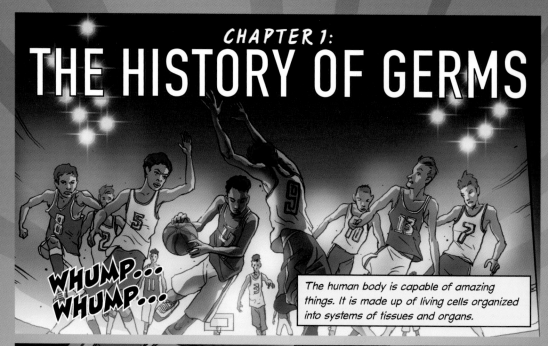

WHUMP...
WHUMP...

The human body is capable of amazing things. It is made up of living cells organized into systems of tissues and organs.

These systems help us in many ways. Our hearts and lungs pump blood and oxygen around the body. Our brains receive and send signals. And our stomachs digest food.

But our bodies are also home to invaders known as germs.

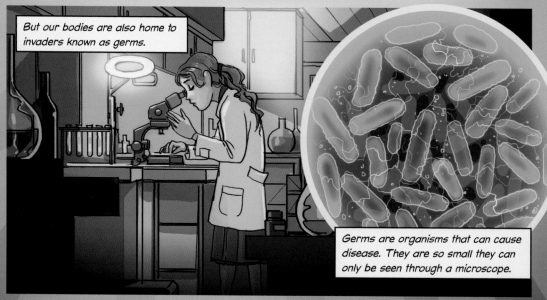

Germs are organisms that can cause disease. They are so small they can only be seen through a microscope.

There are four different types of germs.

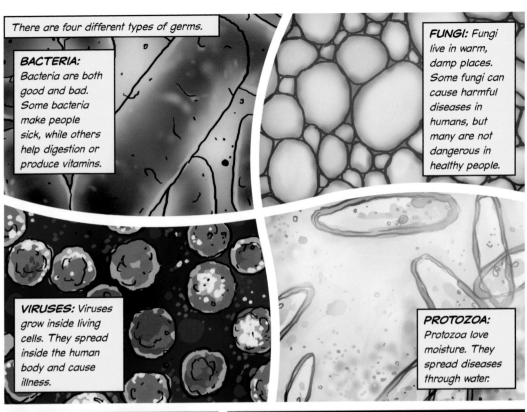

BACTERIA:
Bacteria are both good and bad. Some bacteria make people sick, while others help digestion or produce vitamins.

FUNGI: Fungi live in warm, damp places. Some fungi can cause harmful diseases in humans, but many are not dangerous in healthy people.

VIRUSES: Viruses grow inside living cells. They spread inside the human body and cause illness.

PROTOZOA: Protozoa love moisture. They spread diseases through water.

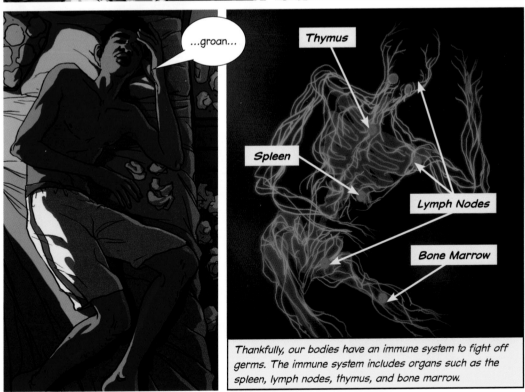

…groan…

Thymus

Spleen

Lymph Nodes

Bone Marrow

Thankfully, our bodies have an immune system to fight off germs. The immune system includes organs such as the spleen, lymph nodes, thymus, and bone marrow.

Before modern medicine, wounds often became infected. This led to serious illnesses. To prevent infection, doctors used substances they found in nature to dress wounds.

In ancient Egypt, people covered burns with honey. The honey acted as a natural bandage to protect the wound from harmful bacteria.

In fourteenth-century Europe, a bacterial infection called the bubonic plague killed tens of millions. Fleas carried bacteria, spreading the infection. People of the time didn't understand bacteria or where the disease came from.

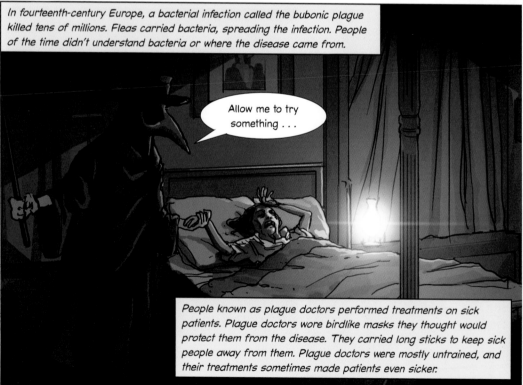

Allow me to try something . . .

People known as plague doctors performed treatments on sick patients. Plague doctors wore birdlike masks they thought would protect them from the disease. They carried long sticks to keep sick people away from them. Plague doctors were mostly untrained, and their treatments sometimes made patients even sicker.

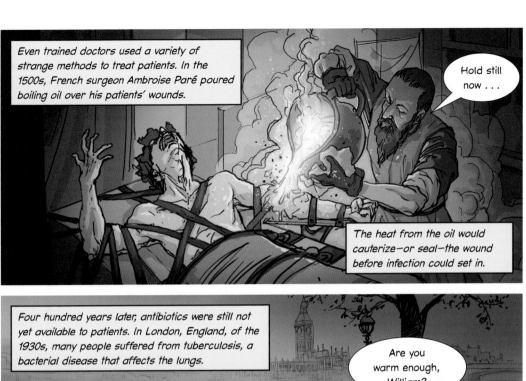

Even trained doctors used a variety of strange methods to treat patients. In the 1500s, French surgeon Ambroise Paré poured boiling oil over his patients' wounds.

Hold still now . . .

The heat from the oil would cauterize—or seal—the wound before infection could set in.

Four hundred years later, antibiotics were still not yet available to patients. In London, England, of the 1930s, many people suffered from tuberculosis, a bacterial disease that affects the lungs.

Are you warm enough, William?

Tuberculosis spreads through the air, such as when people cough and sneeze. Doctors often treated the infection with nothing more than fresh air.

We help our sick patients as best as we can, but we simply can't find a way to treat the illness itself.

COUGH... COUGH...

That was until antibiotics became an option.

But what exactly is an antibiotic?

Antibiotics are medications that stop bacterial infections from copying themselves and multiplying. Antibiotics attack the bacterial cells while avoiding healthy human cells.

Many antibiotics are chemicals found in nature. Fungi and bacteria create them in soil, and scientists produce versions to use for medical treatments.

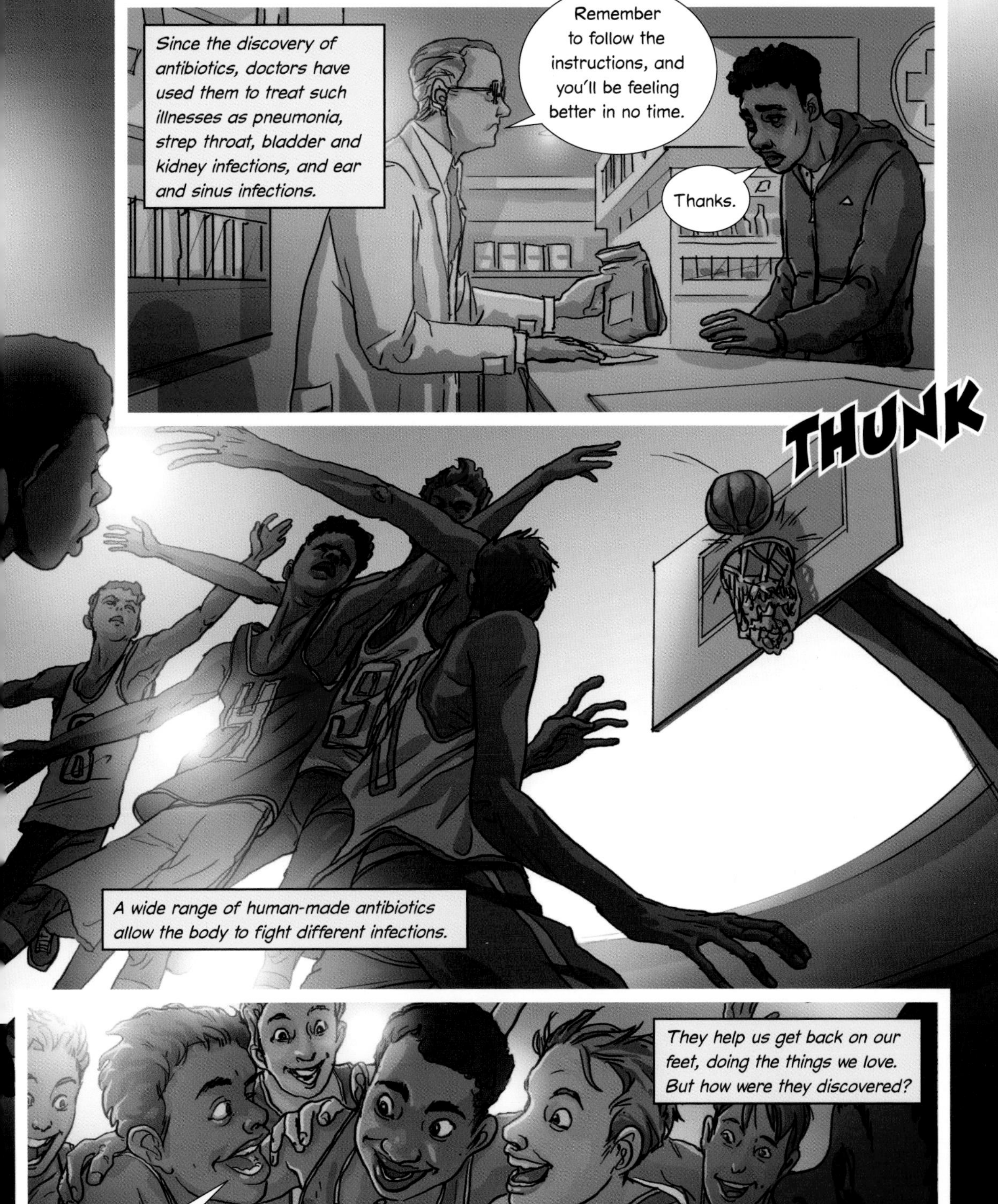
Since the discovery of antibiotics, doctors have used them to treat such illnesses as pneumonia, strep throat, bladder and kidney infections, and ear and sinus infections.
Remember to follow the instructions, and you'll be feeling better in no time.
Thanks.
THUNK
A wide range of human-made antibiotics allow the body to fight different infections.
They help us get back on our feet, doing the things we love. But how were they discovered?
Great shot!

CHAPTER 2:
THE FIRST ANTIBIOTICS

In the nineteenth century, illness caused much human suffering.

The doctor will be in to check on you soon.

COUGH... COUGH...

Infections such as tuberculosis, pneumonia, and whooping cough were often fatal.

Doctors and scientists were searching for better ways to treat their patients.

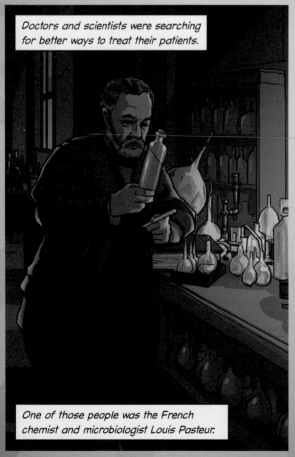

One of those people was the French chemist and microbiologist Louis Pasteur.

As a microbiologist, Pasteur studied microbes such as bacteria.

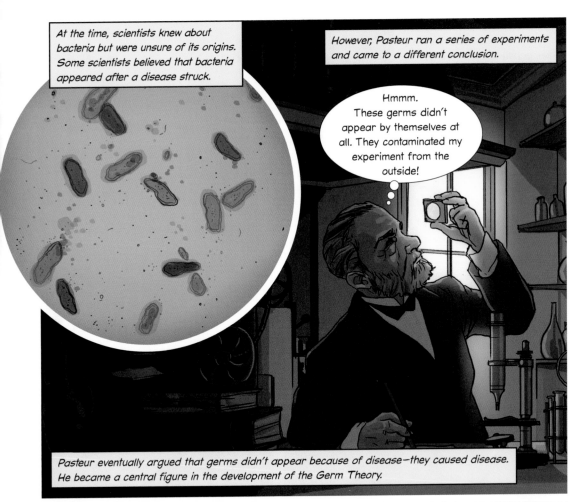

At the time, scientists knew about bacteria but were unsure of its origins. Some scientists believed that bacteria appeared after a disease struck.

However, Pasteur ran a series of experiments and came to a different conclusion.

Hmmm. These germs didn't appear by themselves at all. They contaminated my experiment from the outside!

Pasteur eventually argued that germs didn't appear because of disease—they caused disease. He became a central figure in the development of the Germ Theory.

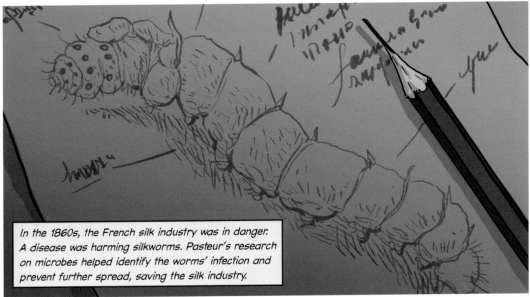

In the 1860s, the French silk industry was in danger. A disease was harming silkworms. Pasteur's research on microbes helped identify the worms' infection and prevent further spread, saving the silk industry.

Scientists also used this new understanding of microbes to keep milk from spoiling.

MOO

FSSHH

They discovered that heating milk killed bacteria that would otherwise spoil it. This method was named pasteurization in honor of Pasteur.

Pasteur's Germ Theory changed the way scientists saw microbes. They knew that certain bacteria caused specific diseases. They also knew that different bacteria lived in different environments.

Oscar, now that we know what we are looking for, we can search for and target harmful bacteria.

Indeed. That will help us find a way to fight them.

In the 1890s, German doctors Rudolf Emmerich and Oscar Loew isolated germs from infected bandages. After studying the germs, they created a medication named pyocyanase. This is considered to be the first scientist-produced antibiotic.

Alas, it has not healed. In fact, it looks worse!

For a brief time, doctors used pyocyanase. Although it helped some patients, it was ineffective for many others. In some cases, it was even poisonous!

BOOM!
BA-DOOM!

Quickly! We have to get him to a medic!

Alexander Fleming was a bacteriologist with Britain's Royal Army Medical Corps during World War I.

In a makeshift laboratory in Boulogne, France, he studied wound infections. Fleming learned that keeping wounds clean and dry was the most effective way to help them heal.

Most doctors at the time used substances called antiseptics to prevent infection. Fleming's experiments proved they did not work well on deep wounds.

But it wasn't Fleming's bravery during World War I that led to his most famous discovery. It was his messiness!

CHAPTER 3:
MESSY MOLDS TO MEDICAL MIRACLE

In August 1928, Alexander Fleming left his lab in London to go on vacation. He planned to return to his work two weeks later.

He left his experiments on the bacteria staphylococcus, a microbe that causes the illness pneumonia, on his workbench.

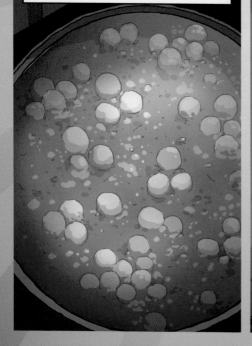

When Fleming returned from his vacation, he noticed something odd about the samples he'd left behind.

Dear me. What is this?

Mold had grown on the bacterial samples. The bacteria near the mold had died. The mold, identified as penicillium, had killed them!

The mold seems to have affected the bacteria.

One sometimes finds what one is not looking for.

Completely by accident, Fleming had discovered the world's first bacteria killer. It was a medical revolution.

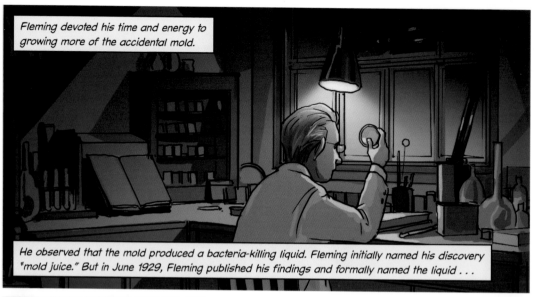

Fleming devoted his time and energy to growing more of the accidental mold.

He observed that the mold produced a bacteria-killing liquid. Fleming initially named his discovery "mold juice." But in June 1929, Fleming published his findings and formally named the liquid . . .

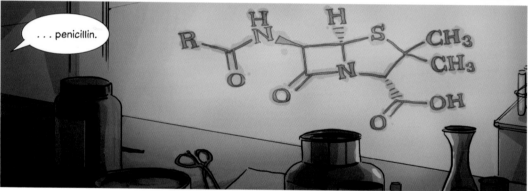

. . . penicillin.

It was another decade before penicillin went from laboratory test substance to life-saving drug.

Howard Florey, a pathologist from the University of Oxford in England, would help lead this development.

By 1940, Florey had hired nearly a dozen scientists to research turning penicillin into a medication. One of those scientists was biochemist Ernst Chain.

I'm looking forward to working with you, Dr. Florey.

Let's hope you're up to the task. Penicillin is notoriously difficult to work with.

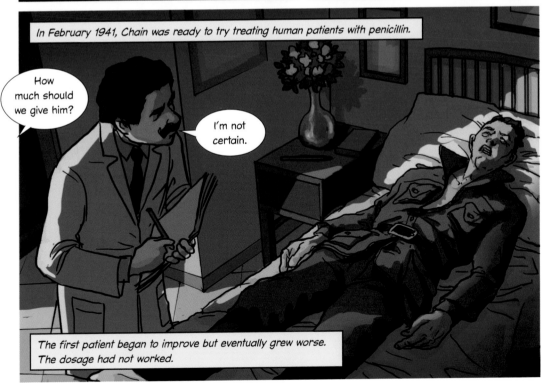

In February 1941, Chain was ready to try treating human patients with penicillin.

How much should we give him?

I'm not certain.

The first patient began to improve but eventually grew worse. The dosage had not worked.

Early uses of penicillin had not been successful. But this changed on February 14, 1942, when a woman named Anne Miller was admitted to a hospital in New Haven, Connecticut. Miller had suffered a miscarriage. Shortly after, she fell ill and was rushed to intensive care.

She has such a high fever. It could be septicemia.

105°

Dr. John Bumstead diagnosed Miller with septicemia, a bacterial infection of the blood.

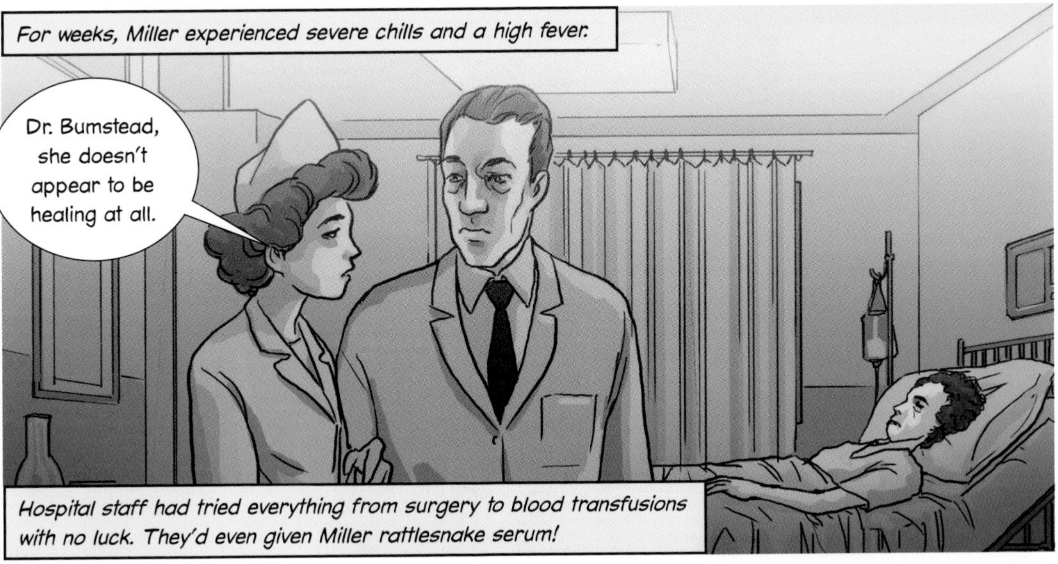
For weeks, Miller experienced severe chills and a high fever.
Dr. Bumstead, she doesn't appear to be healing at all.
Hospital staff had tried everything from surgery to blood transfusions with no luck. They'd even given Miller rattlesnake serum!

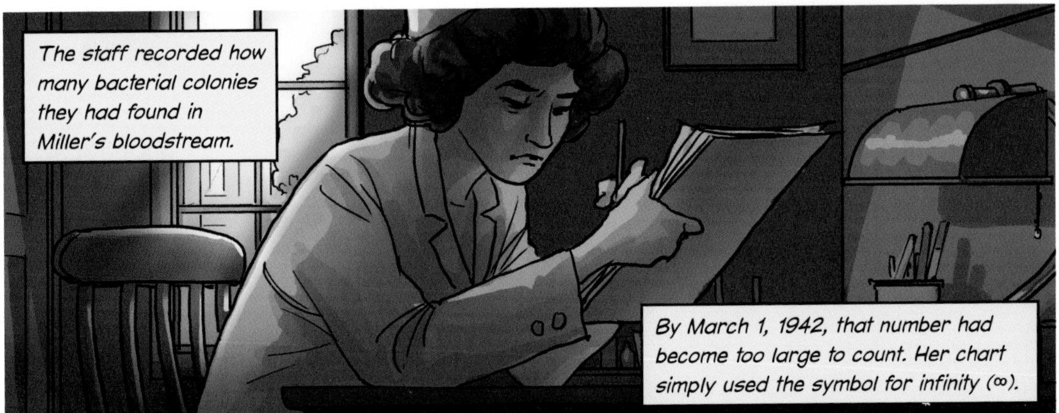
The staff recorded how many bacterial colonies they had found in Miller's bloodstream.
By March 1, 1942, that number had become too large to count. Her chart simply used the symbol for infinity (∞).

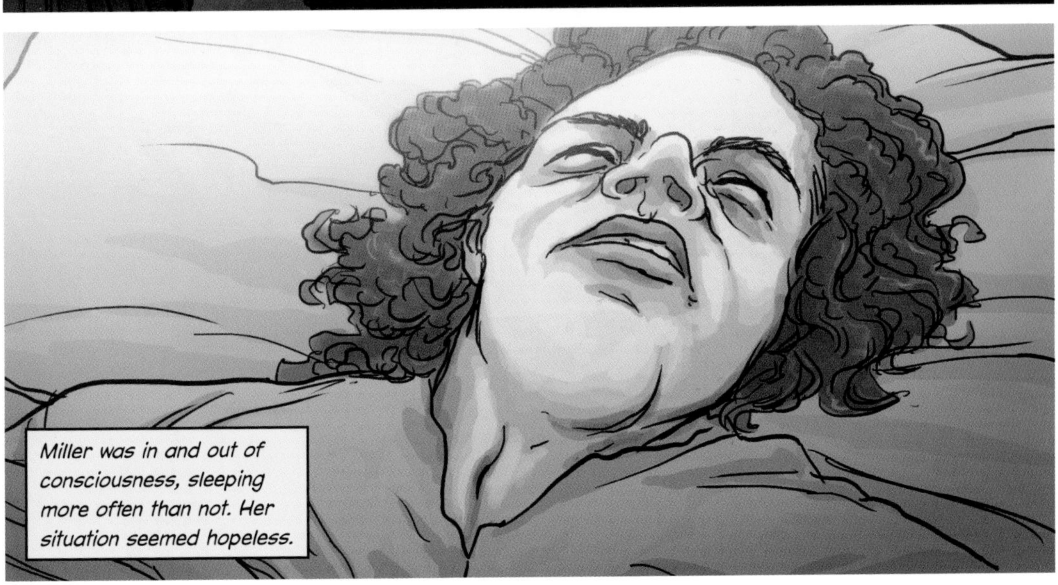
Miller was in and out of consciousness, sleeping more often than not. Her situation seemed hopeless.

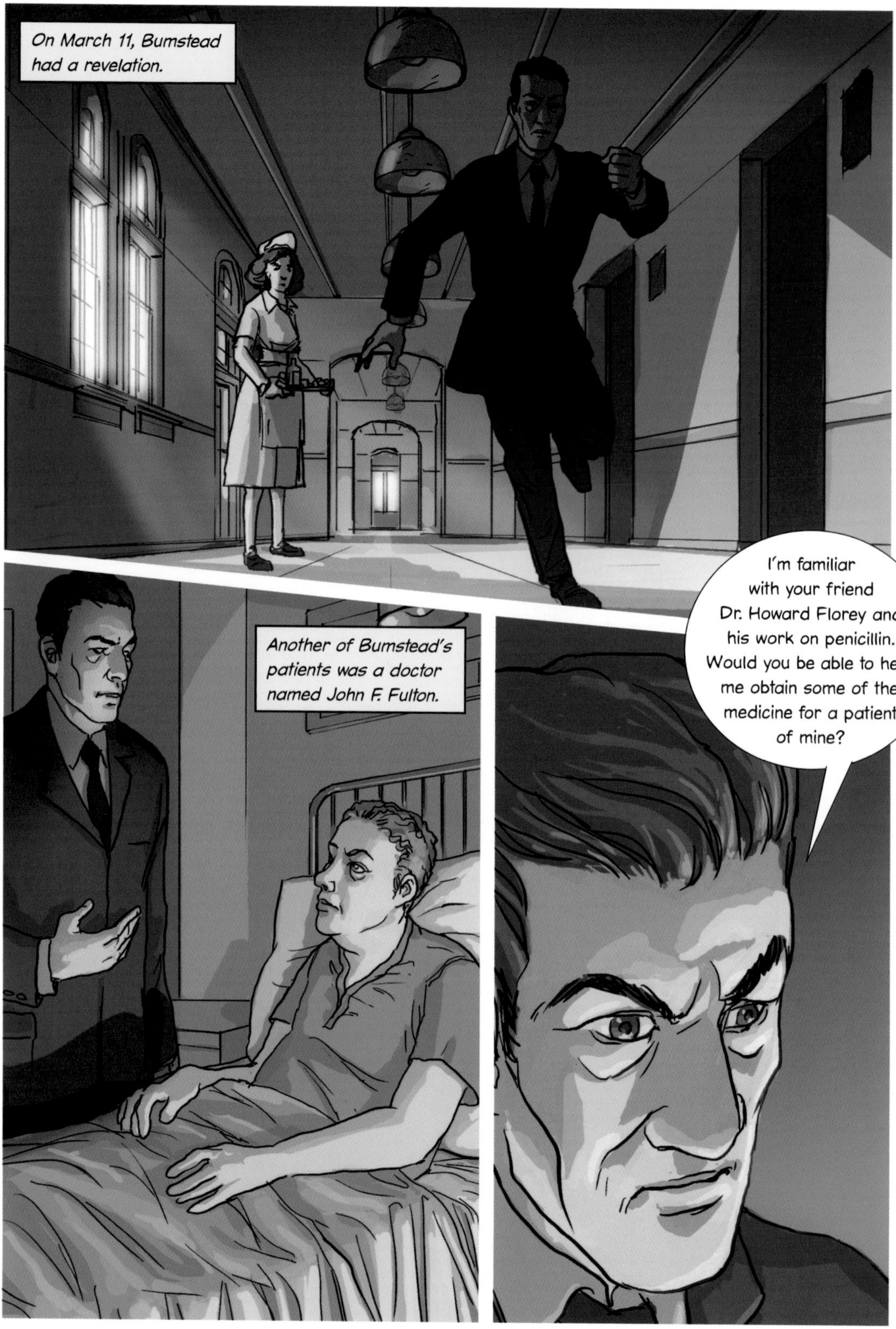
On March 11, Bumstead had a revelation.
Another of Bumstead's patients was a doctor named John F. Fulton.
I'm familiar with your friend Dr. Howard Florey and his work on penicillin. Would you be able to help me obtain some of the medicine for a patient of mine?

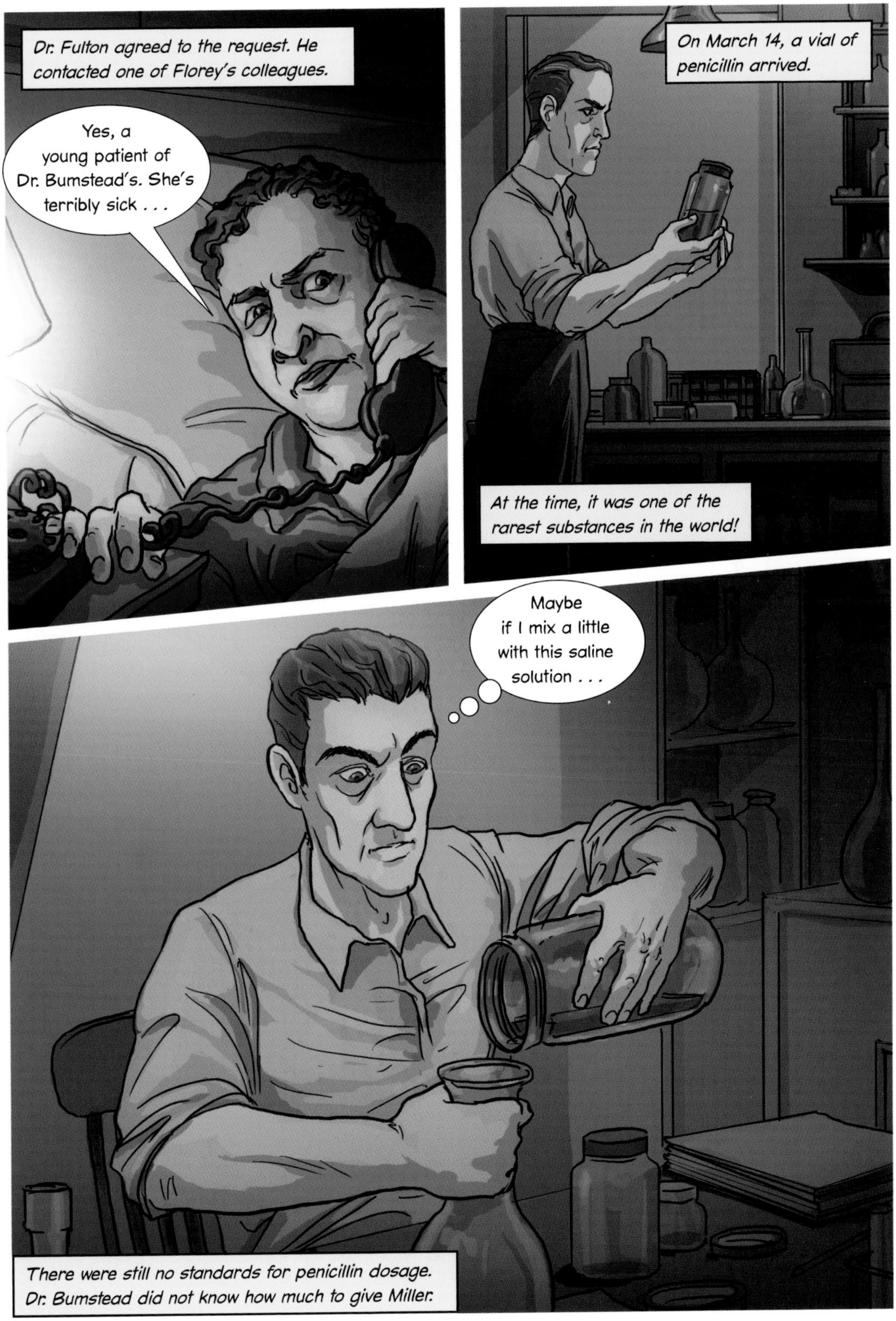
Dr. Fulton agreed to the request. He contacted one of Florey's colleagues.
Yes, a young patient of Dr. Bumstead's. She's terribly sick . . .
On March 14, a vial of penicillin arrived.
At the time, it was one of the rarest substances in the world!
Maybe if I mix a little with this saline solution . . .
There were still no standards for penicillin dosage. Dr. Bumstead did not know how much to give Miller.

Anne Miller received her first dose of penicillin on that day. It was a test dose to see if the medicine would work.

We'll continue to administer a dose every four hours.

Within a day, Miller's temperature dropped. She was even sitting up and eating!

Anne Miller was the fifth person to receive a treatment of penicillin, and the first whose life it saved. She would go on to live another 57 years.

Shortly after being released from the hospital, Anne Miller met Alexander Fleming, the man whose discovery saved her life.

At the same time doctors began using penicillin on human patients, World War II was raging. The team in Oxford speculated that penicillin could help those wounded in the war.

BOOM!

Take cover!

In 1941, the team reached out to the US government. They wanted to mass produce penicillin to support the war effort.

From a lab in Peoria, Illinois, a team of scientists made enough of the drug to help the Allies. Penicillin saved thousands of lives during the war.

Penicillin
THE NEW LIFE-SAVING DRUG

Saves Soldiers' Lives!

Men who might have died will live...if YOU

Give this job Everything You've got!

TIME
THE WEEKLY NEWSMAGAZINE

A Time magazine cover story on May 15, 1944, celebrated Alexander Fleming. The article stated that "Penicillin will save more lives than war spends."

CHAPTER 4:
A WORLD BEYOND PENICILLIN

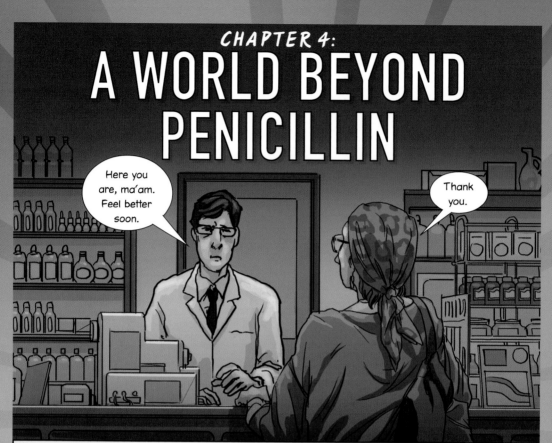

Here you are, ma'am. Feel better soon.

Thank you.

After the war, penicillin became more available to the public. Doctors used it to treat illnesses such as pneumonia, blood and ear infections, and meningitis. Some of these illnesses would have otherwise been dangerous or fatal.

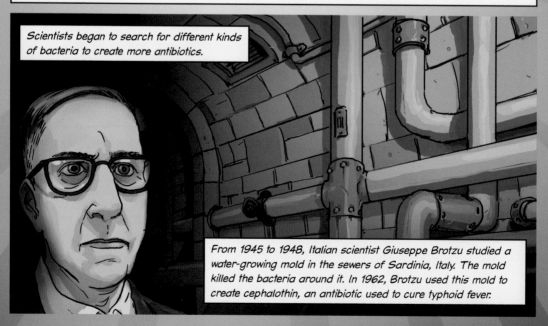

Scientists began to search for different kinds of bacteria to create more antibiotics.

From 1945 to 1948, Italian scientist Giuseppe Brotzu studied a water-growing mold in the sewers of Sardinia, Italy. The mold killed the bacteria around it. In 1962, Brotzu used this mold to create cephalothin, an antibiotic used to cure typhoid fever.

Researchers also found bacteria in soil, a natural environment in which bacteria break down dead organisms.

Half of all commonly used drugs were discovered between the years 1950 and 1960.

During this time, scientists created nearly 80 percent of all antibiotics using the soil-based bacteria streptomyces.

In addition to penicillin and cephalothin, another important antibiotic is amoxicillin. Amoxicillin is a synthetic antibiotic. Scientists created it by changing the chemical makeup of penicillin.

Amoxicillin was developed in 1972 by Beecham Laboratories in the UK.

Amoxicillin

Doctors also began prescribing the antibiotic Amoxil in 1972.

These capsules will help with your strep throat.

Modern drug companies hire teams of scientists to research antibiotics. It's a multibillion-dollar industry.

Every year, doctors prescribe an estimated 154 million orders of antibiotics. But only 70 percent of these are medically necessary.

This is because doctors sometimes mistake viral infections for bacterial infections. Antibiotics cannot kill viruses, so the medication does not help.

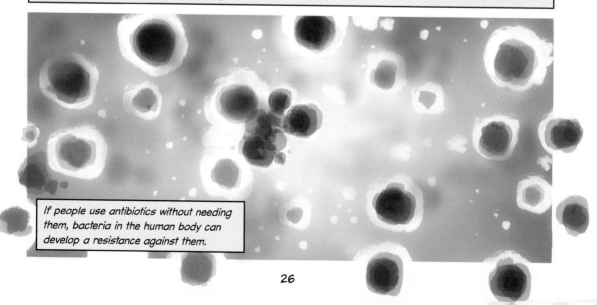

If people use antibiotics without needing them, bacteria in the human body can develop a resistance against them.

This resistance also builds when a bacterial infection is only partially treated. Sometimes patients begin to feel better and stop taking an antibiotic. This kills most of the harmful bacteria but leaves stronger, more resistant bacteria alive.

Remember, you need to take these for the full week to completely kill the infection.

Medicine is losing its power due to the misuse and overuse of antibiotics. More than 2.8 million antibiotic-resistant infections occur in the United States each year.

Doctors call these drug-resistant bacteria superbugs. Infections caused by superbugs last longer and are harder to treat.

When Alexander Fleming gave his Nobel Prize acceptance speech in 1945, he warned people about resistance to antibiotics.

The time may come when penicillin can be bought by anyone in the shops. Then there is the danger that the ignorant man may easily underdose himself and by exposing his microbes to non-lethal quantities of the drug make them resistant.

While the future of antibiotics is uncertain, penicillin alone has saved more than 200 million lives. Its impact on the field of medicine is undeniable.

Doctors continue to study resistant bacteria and find ways to improve antibiotics. But everyone can combat the spread of germs.

Washing hands thoroughly, covering the nose while sneezing, and staying home from school when sick with a fever make an impact too. We can all help fight the battle against harmful bacteria.